THE OTHER SIX DAYS

RELIGIOUS REFLECTIONS

PAUL GRIFFIN

PUBLISHED BY LYON AND LAMB

c/o 22 Trevellan Road, Mylor Bridge,
Falmouth, TR11 5NE

First published 2013
This edition 2017

Available from www.lulu.com/shop

ISBN: 978-0-9527781-8-9

The book is dedicated to the life and work of St Mary's church in Huntingfield, Suffolk where Paul's father-in-law was Rector, where Paul himself was married, where he worshipped and preached, and in whose churchyard he now lies.

The cross above is taken from a photograph of a fragment of 10th century Saxon stonework found close to the church.

The *Other Six Days* was found amongst his papers after Paul's death and has been transcribed, lightly edited and published by his family.

Seven whole days, not one in seven,
I will praise thee;
In my heart, though not in heaven,
I can raise thee.
Small it is, in this poor sort
To enroll thee:
E'en eternity's too short
To extol thee.

From *King of Glory, King of Peace*
George Herbert, 1633

PREFACE

1

Long ago, my wife and I lived with a marvellous couple who were as generous as they were devoted. Every now and then they drew out money they could ill afford, to buy us an object so hideous yet so expensive that it required grace just to accept it, and self-control not to twitch a bit in doing so. Not everyone has the simple gift of receiving gifts: there are those who not only accept them ungracefully, but then proceed quickly to give them away again, or stash them in a drawer unopened and decline to use them. We wanted not to be that sort of person, and I hope we managed it; but it was hard going.

It must be hard going for God at the Eucharist when a succession of people offer their gifts to him, and for the same reason. A week or more of ill-judged effort, its cost greater than its achievement, must call on all God's divine power to accept without a twitch or two. Love makes it possible, as my wife must reflect when I hand her all my dirty clothes at the end of a week, in the hope that she will wash them and darn them and return them to me.

The *Book of Common Prayer* includes the words at the Communion Service: 'Here we offer and present unto thee, O Lord, ourselves, our souls and bodies ...' At which we believe God does not say 'Yuk!' but accepts what he is offered, and gives us grace in return. This is certainly more than we deserve. In return for a load of wasted hours and acts of indifferent quality, he passes us a shining hoard of hours and days and opportunities. He can have no high expectation of what he is likely to receive back at the next Eucharist. Our Lord himself expressed the variety of response in his story about the talents.

There is, of course, variety also in some of the gifts we receive. Paul pointed this out when he talked about diversities of gifts. Though he did not in the least imply that each person was to receive only one gift, he was making the point that there are some gifts that a person will not be given. This is important and true, but can mislead us into

underestimating the extent of the gifts we receive from God every time
we make our Communion.

2

Earthly life seems to consist in making the best use of the gifts we
receive from God, the grace that permits us to function as free human
beings. I am sure that God does not choose to limit his giving to the
Eucharist, but it is on that service that our life seems to many of us to
centre.

What the service is, apart from an attempt to obey our Lord's
command, has been the subject of many writings. The various names by
which it is called shed some light on it. Communion, I think, indicates
the contact between two worlds, the real one and this we call real on
earth. It probably also has a hint of the old word 'commons', meaning a
general meal. The Lord's Supper is an indication of the event of which,
in the words of the old service, we make a memorial. Eucharist, which is
ancient Greek, or modern, for that matter, means 'thank you', and refers
not only to our own attitude to Christ, but also to our Lord's attitude to
the Father. We read that when he took bread, he broke it, and gave
thanks.

But what about the old word, Mass? Can we extract a useful meaning
from that? At first, it seems not. The word comes from the fact that at the
end of the Latin service, the priest used to say: '*Ite, missa est*'; which
means: 'Go, you are dismissed.' On the face of it, this is an authoritarian
remark of the sort that makes a Protestant feel his worst views of Roman
Catholicism are justified. We used to behave like that in British India.
'*Ijazat hai*' - 'You have permission to go'- we would say to a subordinate
when we were fed up with talking to him. I shall not waste time
defending that; though I could do so.

In fact, what the priest is saying is more like: 'Go: you are sent out.'
This is a very Protestant remark, because it implies evangelism. It also
raises the very question I want to explore in these pages, which is how
we can best keep ourselves in a state of grace between Communions.

I suppose we operate like one of those Japanese hand warmers I use
when I am fishing on the beach at night. You shake them up a bit, and
they go hot, so that your hands are warmed. We are shaken up a bit in

the Eucharist, and sent out to foster and communicate the heat that results.

How are we to do it, during the other six days?

I have listed under five headings the sort of life I believe we should lead in consequence of our Sunday Eucharists. The headings, Prayer, Stability, Almsgiving, Light, and Morality, actually form the word PSALM, which may be mildly helpful. These are among the gifts that we can return hopefully to our Father on the following Sunday, and carry away from the altar rail in a new and shining state.

PRAYER

1

'Goodbye; keep in touch,' we say to our friends, and sail off into the other preoccupations of life; until Christmas, when we remember to send a card. With friends, this way of behaviour is inevitable and even healthy; with God, it is plain crazy. It proceeds from a false comparison of a human friend, who has location in place and time, to God, who says: 'Lo, I am with you always.'

There is a genuine mystery here, because if we believe in the special presence of God in the Eucharist, there must be a sense in which there is a special absence of God everywhere else. This is really so, as far as we ourselves are concerned, because it is humanly impossible for us to concentrate on God all through our daily lives. It is not that God is absent from us, but that we, in the sense of which I speak, are absent from him.

As far as we can, we need to keep in touch. Prayer, the first of the characteristics of the Christian life between Communions, is the recovery of touch with God, and can, as we grow expert, become the keeping open of communication.

Much depends on how we see God. To see him in one manifestation is very confining, and false to the doctrine of the Holy Trinity. John Robinson was no doubt right to protest against the idea that God was Up There, but hardly improved matters by calling him the Ground of Being; because a ground is Down There, and open to the same objections. He had just moved God from Up to Down. Similarly, if you see him as the friend always at your side, it means you may cease to regard him as involved in physical matters outside your immediate vicinity. If he is not involved in physical things, what happens to the Old Testament? The God that talked to Gideon was very much involved in things: he not only advised Gideon on the size of his army, but personally introduced an element of chaos into the Midianite camp.

You can say in a lordly way that primitive people saw God wherever they saw mystery: that to Gideon the mystery was how to win battles, so that he saw God in that way; but that we have grown up since then. This is true enough. If you live in a mountainous area, the mountain tops are very mysterious, and tend to turn your mind to God. Moses climbed a mountain to collect the Commandments. Again, if you are wandering in the wilderness and living in tents, you may make your own mystery by having a tent where no one is allowed to go, and calling it the Ark of the Lord. If you are in an area where earthquakes or tornadoes occur, you may say God is in the earthquakes or tornadoes. Later, perhaps, when you settle in Israel, you may see God in the lilies of the field, the ephemeral flowers that come up in the morning and die by evening, like Morning Glory.

The very talk about God being Up There was because of the abiding mystery of the stars; and surely the mystery of matter is somewhere behind our talk of the Real Presence of Christ, as it was behind John Robinson's talk about the Ground of Being.

God must, in some way beyond our understanding, be involved in all these things, though he is not to be identified with them. Gideon and Moses and the rest were quite right to think that God was involved in mysteries; but they were wrong if they thought that he was limited to mysteries.

Prayer, then, must not try to limit or domesticate God. As C.S. Lewis's hero says, Aslan is not a tame lion. One has the uneasy feeling with certain Protestants that they regard their Lord as a sort of pet trotting at their heels. The Catholic practice of Benediction, worshipping the Real Presence in the Holy Sacrament, perhaps corrects that; but there is truth in both the visions, of God as a friend, and of him as a powerful Lord. Neither is sufficient on its own.

Remembering Gideon, I have some sympathy for the clergymen who assumed God was firing our guns for us in two World Wars. You cannot cut him out of any human activity. We are never completely on our own; but he is always bigger than we imagine.

So in prayer, we have to look for him. Pascal, speaking for God, said: 'Comfort yourself; you would not seek me if you had not found me.'

Yet here, as so often, we are in the presence of paradox; for God reveals himself, and is not to be grasped. The initiative is always with him. What Pascal and I call seeking is in fact not a reaching out so much as a preparation, a readiness to see and understand.

If we decide to take a touring holiday and drive to the Pyrenees, we are likely to do an immense amount of planning, consulting garages about spares and headlamps, badgering the motoring organisations, asking ourselves constantly: 'What shall we do if this or that happens?' This is the sort of preparation I mean: a turning of the mind towards likely events.

On the other hand, if we go somewhere local for the day, probably no such thoughts will bother us. We are likely to jump into the car and drive to our destination, with no spare fan belt, and no anticipation of any unusual event.

In God's world we are always driving into the unknown: to the Pyrenees if you like. The more we have a sense of uniqueness about what we do, a belief that God lies ahead on the road, the more our life can be called prayerful.

Habit deadens us. When we go to a special dinner, we expect to start with grace. When we eat another routine meal, we are less likely to say: 'Lord, bless this food,' and more likely to say: 'Not sausages again!'

Even to unusual events, we may offer stock responses when something more is needed. When General Orde Wingate prepared his troops to cross the river Chindwin, he announced that the password would be: 'One more river,' and the reply: 'And that the river of Jordan.' It was his way of indicating the nature of the adventure on which we were embarking, showing us that it was not just another offensive. Yet three weeks after the start of his greatest adventure, I sat in his Operations Room and looked out over the hills of Assam, and realised the General was dead, somewhere among them. My response was to think: 'The rest of life will be dull now.'

I was wrong. I should have thought: 'God is in this terrible accident too. I must look for him in it, and believe that he will show himself.' If we don't know that God is in death as well as in life, then we haven't thought enough about the Crucifixion.

All this is a part of keeping in touch with God.

2

Keeping in touch involves adopting a prayerful attitude, which does not necessarily mean kneeling down in a quiet place. Rather it means being ready under all circumstances to look beyond the clutter of life for the Master we met at the Eucharist.

The word 'clutter' implies too much, of course. If everything material is to be taken as obscuring God, then bread and wine have to be included; which is absurd. Clutter is something we keep in our lofts: our old stamp collection, the mouth organ we used to play, the old records that once drove our parents mad, stuff we have outgrown. As we grow older, we accumulate more and more clutter, and begin consciously to get rid of it; unless we are like the old lady who refuses to go into sheltered accommodation because she will not be able to keep the sideboard. Even she cannot imagine that she is going to drag the sideboard as far as Peter's gate. We all know that in the end the whole of our earthly trappings will be so much clutter; but in the meanwhile we do value material things, as once we valued our mouth organ, and our records, and our stamp collection. It is not till our last moment on earth that we cease to value bread and wine.

However, when our Lord wanted to institute the Eucharist, he asked for a quiet room with his friends and a simple meal, away from the complications of crowds and the city and human fashion. The place was not for transcendental meditation, or ectoplasmic spiritualism, just for decent people to live in, with space and time to think. This was a sort of withdrawal from the world, but only to concentrate minds on aspects of the world: food, drink, friendship, what to do next. Whatever happened later in the history of the Church, there is no precedent in the Bible for final rejections of the sort common in India, and described in Kipling's wonderful short story, *The Miracle of Purun Bhagat*.

Medieval people, living in bad conditions, tended to assume that when Jesus said: 'This is my body; this is my blood', he was showing man a way to escape from the material world into the world of the spirit; as if the material world was naturally evil. But the material world, however messy, complex, abused, and interpenetrated with evil, is not itself evil. When God made the universe, he saw everything that he had made, and behold, it was good. Jesus may be showing us the way into earthly life, not out of it. He is not only involved in the bread and the wine, he is involved in the lamb, the fish, the harvest, and all else. Talk of the Resurrection of the Body implies that death will not be stronger than our joy in God's creation. After the Resurrection, Jesus serves a meal of fish at the lake side. He eats fish and honey on the road to Emmaus.

So when we go apart, as Jesus went apart, into a quiet place, we do not go in order to reject matter; rather we go in order to look at the giant jigsaw puzzle in which we live, and to discern the hand of God in it. In the temptations in the wilderness Jesus wrestled with spiritual matters, but essentially in order that he might see what was his task in the world: Survival? No. Miracles? No. Power? No.

3

That said, we have to remember that God is a spirit, and that prayer is nothing if it is not spiritual. There is an element of withdrawal from the world in prayer. The point I am making is that the Christian tradition is unlike the Buddhist or Hindu one; it points not towards a Nirvana, but to earthly existence. The monastic orders, however contemplative, exist not for the sake of contemplation itself, but insist that they are for the world's benefit. The waiting upon God is spiritual; the resulting impulse is directed to the world.

When Jacob has his vision of angels in the wilderness, God tells him his purpose in history. The stone on which Jacob lays his head perhaps stands for the stubbornness of material things, which exist even in the wilderness. It may also represent suffering, by the light of which God's ways are made clear.

Jesus chooses a quiet room and simple surroundings; Jacob does not choose, but has a quiet place thrust upon him. This happens to all of us at times, when we are empty, desolate, in pain. At such times the voice may speak that is drowned by the murmur of the central heating, the rustle of notes, and the easy chatter of the disc jockey.

Or we may choose a quiet place, perhaps a Retreat house, with basic comfort, basic food, and silence. Not everyone can cope with Retreats; but everyone needs the equivalent state, in which to wait and listen for the voice of God.

I am conscious of relapsing into the easy language of the professional: 'Why not talk to God as a friend?' they say. Yes and no. No harm in a bit of talking, or a bit of friendship, as long as you do not regard God as either a convenient platform or as only a friend. Then again, the advice to listen may seem to imply that something will eventually come through with a label on it: 'This is God speaking.' Not a bit of it. In prayer, it is truer to say that by degrees we learn to look through God's eyes. I remember a new boy who was unhappy at school saying to me: 'I don't like it, sir; but I know I've got to go through with it.' How did he know? He would say it was something inside him. If I had said: 'That was God speaking to you in your wilderness,' he would have thought I was daft. But it would have been true.

The concept of prayer is somewhat confused by the custom of public prayer. This dates back to the Jews, who have always acknowledged public and private prayer. In the time of Jesus, public religious observances took place three times a day morning, afternoon, and evening. The Temple was clearly also used for private prayer, because we are told of two men who went up to pray and used the first person singular: I and me, not we and us. Jesus himself follows both customs.

Similarly, during the week, we have the offices of Morning and Evening Prayer, with Compline for some. Here the community confesses and intercedes, using the first person plural. This is very different from private prayer, the simple being with God; but it may involve an element of that.

The esteemed Methodist writer Neville Ward wrote an alarming but fascinating book called *The Use of Praying*, in which he said that in his view some Christians could manage very nicely without prayer. This exemplifies the sort of confusion that arises from the elasticity of the word. What Neville Ward must have meant was that some Christians can manage without formulating lists of intercessions; without, if you like, making speeches to God as a child is taught to do when he says: 'God bless Mummy and Daddy and Towser and Tabby; and send me a guinea pig.' I can just about agree to that; but the statement is otherwise the reverse of the truth, for praying actually defines a Christian. Surely all of us must have sat in a boat on a rough sea, and held ourselves before God; or faced a death, or a great blessing, and said something to whoever is out there. Surely it follows from our Lord's words on prayer that prayer is the positive recognition of the divine rule. To pray is to accept the Kingdom of God.

Neville Ward says something else that I find difficult: that prayer is not a duty. I can see that it is not only a duty; but if it is not a duty, what else is it? The word 'duty' seems to mean something very nasty to Neville Ward, as I fear it tends to do to all of us. When the Vicar asks us to pray for Muddlecombe-with-Dinglebottom and its incumbent and Readers, I confess my heart sinks. Muddlecombe-with-Dinglebottom is nothing to me; but it is another part of the Body to which we belong, and I know it is my duty to pray for it, even if I do have to stretch myself a bit. If I stick to private prayer, and personal needs, my religion tends to become a 'thee-and-me' affair, and hang the rest.

Even so, the modern habit of reading great lists of objects for intercessions in church, ranging from the Deanery of some West Indian island to the assistants in the local bookshop too easily becomes sanctimonious. It is one thing to will a previously unfelt care, but quite another to pretend to a care you do not feel. Imagine three people saying grace before a meal: one smells the roast lamb and mint sauce and feels the gratitude; another, further from the kitchen, is hungry and dutifully says a blind thanks; the third intensely dislikes lamb, but wants the other two to see he is pious.

A prayer needs to be felt, even with a bit of effort; otherwise we are creating a film of religiosity under which lies nothing. Sanctimoniousness is very destructive, of a person, or of a Church.

4

Luke says that Jesus wanted people to keep on praying, and not to give up (Luke 18.1). If we identify prayer with silent meditation, we know this is not possible; but in reality there are so many ways of prayer that more goes on than one might imagine. Some people do keep on praying. They chatter away to God all day long, grumbling at him, asking him for things, thanking him sometimes. It is not an ideal attitude to regard God as someone to natter to when there is no one else about, but it has respectable roots, and it certainly keeps in touch. The old Greek lady I sat with on a long bus journey in Western Greece was doing something similar, because every time we passed a church I saw her lips move as she crossed herself. It was the continuation of a conversation begun somewhere quiet and dark, in front of a Greek icon.

But some of this so-called prayer is really talking not to God, but to ourselves. We acquire from radio and television the idea that time only exists to be filled with talk, and we feel obscurely guilty when we are silent, as if we are being boring. That I presume is why the TV commentator tells us Boris Becker is serving when we can see that plainly enough. Bores in fact are not silent people at all, and although God is not easily bored, I feel sure he does not mind silence. To me, a real friend is one with whom I can sit silently. To kneel down in church, to bless God for his goodness, plead our unworthiness, and then just shut up and lean against him is a great treat. It is perfectly possible to find moments, even during activity, when something similar is possible.

A habit formed in church can often be carried out into daily life in this way; but it needs to be formed first; which is one reason why we have Parish Quiet Days and Retreats. Twentieth century men and women are frightened by these. Just as one is alarmed to be told by one's spouse to 'tell them that story about the Englishman and the Scotsman', because one has forgotten how it went, so one is alarmed to be told: 'Now pray.'

It is like being in primary jungle. The noise and the chatter, the movement and the singing, are up at the tops of the trees; but they are all nourished and sustained in the dark silent forest floor here a hundred feet down, where the roots grow in the deep soil. You are away from the monkeys and parakeets, and you know that something is expected of you; but what and how?

Time solves this for you. Patrick Leigh Fermor, describing the first time he was left alone in a monastery, wrote: 'I had asked for quiet and solitude and peace, and here it was. It began to rain over the woods outside, and a mood of depression and unspeakable loneliness suddenly felled me like a hammer stroke.' But gradually, as he put it: 'I lost the sensation of being by mistake locked up in a catacomb.' He found himself in a strange new world, timeless and offering a great peace and exaltation.

It is useless to pretend that this world can be taken into ordinary life, among the traffic and television, up at the top of the trees; but some of its habits can be taken; as when in a tremendous crisis, when you feel defeated, you may know how to lean against somebody or something, not explaining, not even asking, rather as it says in the Baptismal Service: 'I turn to God.'

I have not said more than a fraction of all that is to be said about prayer. I am sure each person has different ways and experiences; and though it is good to read the thoughts on the subject of a truly spiritual person, some may well lead one unnecessarily to despair of one's own practice. There are prayer bores, who are always using the word. 'I've prayed about it,' they tell you unnecessarily when they want to get their way. 'I'm praying for you,' they say in order to appear one up over you. I would advise anyone seldom to talk about prayer, but always to practise it. It is the stuff of life, the prime way to keep in touch with God.

STABILITY

1

Variety, they say, is the spice of life; but variety of faith can be a pretty dangerous spice. It is good to see God in different aspects - what else is the Holy Trinity about? - but losing sight of him for long or short spells, however common an experience, brings us into all sorts of danger.

Ordinary sin is the obvious example. On the face of it, stealing or hating or committing adultery does not always involve losing sight of God. We may speak to God in the very act, saying, for example: 'I know you disapprove of this, God; but I must do it. I need to.' We are deceiving ourselves: a cloud has gone across the sun, because if God were really in sight, the act would be unthinkable. To envisage it as we came away from the Eucharist in a state of grace would or should have been impossible. The problem is to hold on to faith at its full strength, to achieve stability in the face of the distractions and temptations around.

One of these is mass emotion, which surrounds us powerfully and invisibly in the form of culture, and just as powerfully but more visibly on particular occasions. Isaiah speaks of our going astray like sheep, and then adds with less than his usual acumen that this means we have turned everyone to his own way. He had not been watching sheepdog trials; for sheep seldom turn to their own way. When there is one who splits off from the rest, you can see it is not a desire for independence, by his eagerness to return as soon as possible to the familiar mob.

I have come out of a play or a concert and heard one person say: 'How marvellous!' and another person say: 'How rotten!' Yet once they are aware of each other's views, their opinions tend to converge, and become similar. Is it because they learn from each other? or because they are anxious to be in the same flock?

Certainly, in a confined space or a large crowd, opinions do tend towards unanimity. You can feel the pressure of mass emotion upon you. If you had been there when Mark Antony spoke to the Roman crowd after Julius Caesar's death, it would have been very difficult not to want to murder the conspirators. Equally, when Billy Graham was in his prime, it was difficult for anyone in his audience not to want to be a Christian. Can we say that mass emotion is always a bad thing?

Perhaps one must take refuge in saying that it depends. Just as a drug may operate for a good or bad purpose, so may mass emotion; both are inevitable, but neither is to be taken lightly. Culture itself is largely an unconscious process: no one seems to have been manipulating the mob who shouted 'Hosanna!' when Jesus entered Jerusalem; they were prepared by their upbringing to cheer the Messiah. Even the mob who shouted for him to be crucified were exercising a reasonably free, if disastrous, choice for Barabbas. You can argue about whether the two mobs were the same, but it is likely that they included many people in common. These people are a prime example of instability, of failure to hold on to faith.

Anyone who has served on a Diocesan Synod knows something about mass emotion. The Bishop stands up towards the end of a crucial debate which looks like going the wrong way, and you can suddenly feel opinion changing. The later it is, and the more tired and emotional the members, the more volatile the mood. Long ago, I came to the conclusion that the constant identification of this process with the Holy Spirit is quite wrong. The Spirit may use mass emotion to his good ends, but it is highly dangerous to hold him responsible for what is often sentimentality. Mass emotion in itself is dangerous and unreliable, causing the very instability against which we must be on guard.

I have not forgotten Pentecost, when the outpouring of the Holy Spirit was neither dangerous nor unreliable. If you look closely at the account in Acts, you will find that the crowd on that day was divided: 'They were all amazed, and in doubt, saying one to another: What meaneth this? Others mocking said: These men are full of new wine.' That is not a description of mob emotion.

And after Peter's sermon at Pentecost, we hear: 'They that gladly received his word were baptised.' It presumably follows that those who did not receive his word gladly were not baptised. Not much hysteria there.

19

Christ did not come to make us unanimous. 'I am come,' he says, 'to set a man at variance with his own father, and the daughter against her mother, and the daughter-in-law against the mother-in-law' (Matt 10.35). It is a hard saying, but it is there. Stability may involve being apparently out of step.

2

Uncertainty is a normal condition of our life. We think we are going to do something, and it all goes wrong. We go to the dentist's, and find the electricity has failed, or the dentist has contracted flu. We go to the airport to catch a plane, and find we face three hours on the tarmac.

Even in science, where everything is supposed to be cut and dried, a Mr Heisenberg has stated an Uncertainty Principle, which assures us how little we can really know about where a particle is, and how fast it is travelling.

Twenty-four years ago I said publicly of space travel, as anyone at that time was in a position to say: 'Somewhere, some time, a circuit will be imperfect, a fixing will work loose, there will be overheating, radio silence, failure to fire; and men will die.' Years later, the uncertainty principle I had stated was vividly brought home by the deaths of four Americans in the Challenger capsule. British Rail alone convinces us that in life we can be certain of only one thing: uncertainty.

And yet, and yet … We do eventually get our teeth seen to, we do eventually travel by air or rail; spacecraft are still operating, and we do seem to be able to continue our study of particles, despite Mr Heisenberg.

We have to look on the bright side. I am writing, as no doubt you are reading, in a building that has not yet collapsed, breathing a perfect chemical mixture for the maintenance of life. The upward pressure on us from seat and floor is exactly equal to our weights acting downwards - otherwise some very odd things would happen - our hearts are beating, livers are palpitating, eyes are blinking regularly. I planned to write this in advance, and here it is. There is a basic efficiency and purpose somewhere.

When I look at the life of our Lord, I can see a pattern of life very like that of our own. He has the same simple certainties that we have: the certainties of natural law; but all the time there are hiccups - in the packed hotels of Bethlehem, in the temptations, in the diseased people around him, the sinful faces, the jockeying for position among the disciples, and in the final disasters. We see a man fighting, fighting against the uncertainties, loving people in spite of themselves, giving us a way by which to live in the same world.

Long ago, when I was trying to run a school, the clergyman I had invited to come and preach at the eleven o'clock service failed to turn up on time. So I left the chaplain to start the service, and went and stood on a cold and windy corner, cursing and waiting for the wretched man to arrive. While I was there, a lovely little seven-year old girl called Alice, who was my respected librarian's granddaughter, came and stood on my shoes. She peered up at me to see if I was worthy of what she was going to say; then she said: 'This is my Grandad's school. Would you like me to show you it?'

Well, in fact it was as much my school as her Grandad's; but the message was clear. There was I, reacting to a hitch with anger; and there was darling Alice, rejoicing in the overall beauty of everything, and wanting to share it with me. I felt terribly ashamed. Yet again, out of the mouth of babes and sucklings had come truth.

Alice was loving, and I was not. She was positive, and I was negative. 'Whosoever shall not receive the Kingdom of God as a little child shall in no wise enter therein' (Luke 18.17).

A dangerous certainty can be a great cause of instability and failure of faith; its brother uncertainty is as great an enemy.

3

When an electric current passes through a wire, its energy is dissipated by something called resistance, which generates heat. When God's will passes through human beings, there is a similar phenomenon. I presume that angels are cool creatures, perfect conductors of God's word; but we are not angels.

Full of some virtuous intention, I drive to the nearest shopping town in foul weather, with the roads crowded. Cars and lorries have their lights on, and flash them at me. My windscreen is covered in mud, and so is my virtuous intention. Uncertainty gnaws at me and fills me with a false certainty: that everyone in the world is mad, bad, and dangerous except myself.

I reach the shops, and find them packed with the variety and colour of the human race. A pushchair is driven hard into my ankle. The owner looks over my shoulder with glazed eyes, and speaks to someone behind me. A scream breaks out nearby, where a mother is holding her child's arm and shaking it viciously. Curiously, it is the mother, not the child, who is screaming. Everyone seems to be quarrelling, sulking, bashing into each other. I can find no one at the sales counter of the big store, though two girls are patting their hair and chatting over by the wall.

Aware that I am in a dangerous mood, I try to pray. My first thought is of incredulity that Jesus could die for that lot. Then I begin to suspect that the angels are bellowing their heads off, telling me that I am a part of all this, asking me why I should not open doors for people, help them with their pushchairs, reminding me that goodness can spread fast. But my resistance to mediating God's will at this point is strong, and generates heat in the form of guilt and irritation. My only hope is to find quiet, concentrate, then try again with a clearer spiritual windscreen.

So which is worse, going with the crowd, or reacting against it? Life does seem very difficult sometimes; and just to make it worse, we need to remember the danger of separating ourselves from it: like the little girl who wrote: 'God loves everyone who is good like me and my friend Lucy, but not people like Gillian who take other people's pencils.' The ivory tower of self-righteousness is built upon irritation.

When Jesus found himself in a crowd, he tended to make a healing gesture: he walked quietly away and said nothing, performed a cure, told a story, or, with the five thousand, fed them. We can follow him, but we always follow a long way behind. Paul has sensible advice here, reminding us that we all have limitations. 'If it be possible,' he says, 'as much as lies in you, live peaceably with all men.' The 'if' is important.

Suppose it is not possible; suppose it does not lie in me? The wise answer is to keep away. If the meat is too strong for your stomach, leave it alone. We cannot all cope with everything.

Meanwhile, we should not write off anyone on God's behalf, just because we cannot cope with them. He made everyone good, however strong their tendency to evil. How the struggle goes within them is between themselves and God. It is part of the recovery of our own essential goodness to leave other people's goodness alone.

4

There are far greater and more respectable reasons for instability than mass emotion. War, volcanoes, Chernobyl, the Tower of Siloam, the concentration camps, are just a few. They bring the conventional unbeliever to say: 'I live in a universe that has gone wrong, and I cannot believe in a God who can be responsible for such a place.'

Of course, a person who says that sets up his own expectations, and insists that any God would fit in with them. He places himself at the centre of the universe, yet knowing that he cannot change it; indeed, refusing to connect its state with himself. We may not take that view; yet we may still be rocked out of faith by some inexplicable disaster. A casual bomb in war kills hundreds. You can say that it was due to overcrowding, mislocation, and so forth: that a point had to be made, so that matters could be better handled in future. But always we are driven to ask: 'Could the point not have been made less spectacularly?'

The fall of the tower of Siloam, killing eighteen men, raises the issue for all time. It produces a curious remark from Jesus about these men: '... think ye that they were sinners above all men that dwelt in Jerusalem? Nay, but except ye repent, ye shall all likewise perish.' (Luke 13.4-5) This presumably means that catastrophes are not a judgment on those who suffer from them, but that human sin none the less lies behind them. This is borne out by the story of the blind man in St John's Gospel, where Jesus says that catastrophes are a part of God's revelation of himself. I find it hard to believe that the sort of human sin to which Jesus refers is primarily the profiteering or understaffing or inadequate scaffolding which an enquiry may have found to be the cause of the tower's collapse; if only because a natural disaster or a genuine accident may occur without any direct human agency. Rather, he seems to be speaking in a generalised way, to the effect that we sin, and therefore towers fall and men are born blind.

Here indeed is a mystery. We have seen it destroy the faith of believers who happen to be related to victims. To them, it seems cruel to say: 'Except ye repent, ye shall all likewise perish.' Yet this may not be merely a threat of hell fire: the word 'likewise' suggests that we are all going to have a tower fall on us, sooner or later. Yes indeed: the death that overtook those eighteen will come to all of us; and death is a punishment for sin: not our specific sins, but the general state of humanity.

Beyond seeing that the Crucifixion of our Lord is connected with the solution to the problem, we have to leave the problem of evil as a mystery. If we insist on saying that God has cruelly willed the suffering of the world, then we have lost our faith, lost hope, and joy, and the need for repentance. Here is the greatest challenge to our stability.

5

Clinging to the rock, as the Victorian hymn writer put it, is a frequent state. I would however want to add a bit to the metaphor, because God is not only the rock, but the water whose ebb and flow tests the clinger, and in whose richness is the daily food on which we live. If that makes us sound like sea anemones, so be it: it is not a bad metaphor. A sea anemone, like the immortal soul, is a very beautiful thing. When it shuts itself away it becomes no more than a hideous piece of red jelly; but when it waves its tentacles and seizes what is on offer, it becomes a lovely cross between an animal and a flower. Our stability consists not only in hanging on, but in being open to the ebb and flow around us. Grace comes not only in the Eucharist, but also in daily life.

Grace, however it comes, is the food of the spirit, enabling it to live and grow. Just as polluted water can harm marine life, so evil can harm the spirit. Jesus tends to use the metaphor of yeast or leaven, which can be good, as in the fermentation of wine, or bad, as when wild yeasts turn food sour. He compared the idea of holiness of the Pharisees to wild yeast, growing and growing until faith turned sour in legal niceties. He compared the Kingdom of God to good yeast, the tiny living idea that grows like yeast in bread till the whole substance is transformed by it.

Both sorts of yeast seem to be intrinsic in the culture that presses upon us from all sides. When Western missionaries took the Word abroad, they found that it was entangled with racial problems, greed, gluttony, and diseases not apparent before, but apparently coexisting with Christian civilisation. In Northern Ireland and elsewhere, Christ is preached by different communities who often seem hostile to each other. Paul advises us to be thankful in such cases that Christ is preached, however mixed the results, and to trust that in the process of fermentation the good yeast will drive out the bad.

This metaphor makes it clear that we are battle fields of the spirit, neither a comfortable nor a stable condition, and one which may seem to reduce us to passive acceptance. I hope this is where one metaphor breaks down, and we need to return to the other marine one. Clearly a sea anemone will do its best to choose the food that most benefits it, however it may acquire harmful substances in the process. We too retain our free will, to take sides in the fight to survive in a stable form.

ALMSGIVING

1

This will be the shortest section, though not therefore the least important. It will be short because we have all heard so much about Stewardship that we can easily have formed the impression that fund raising is all the Church cares about.

It is quite interesting to see how the Church fares when it is pursuing a line parallel to a fashionable worldly activity. There are many who say it should be 'businesslike', for example. This is fine if efficiency is meant; but not all the methods used in worldly businesses are for us.

Similarly, the methods used to extract money from reluctant people may not all be suitable to the Church, though some of them have undoubtedly helped in increasing revenues. Good teaching should ensure that people are not reluctant. The vital need to give money sacrificially is recognised by Hindus and by Jews, and was recognised by Christians until the sixpence-in-the-plate syndrome did so much damage. Christians, on the other hand, have probably been better at the giving of time and talents, with the life-giving example of their Lord before them.

And, indeed, it is on that example that all our giving must rest. We have to understand giving before we understand almsgiving.

If you go to the dentist with someone you love, you may sit in the waiting room while they are being treated. You hear a low murmur of voices, then silence. Then the dreadful scream starts: wheeee! It goes on and on, and you remember how your husband, wife, child, parent hates and fears the drill. It is a mere step to thinking: 'If only I were having that drill. I know he (or she) can't bear it. It would be so much better if I could sit in that dentist's chair instead, and not pretend to read a magazine outside, with teeth as sound as bells.'

Once, I remember, my wife told me she couldn't concentrate on what was happening to her in the surgery for worrying about my feelings, listening outside the door.

Natural affection breaks down the walls between people in this way, and makes them part of each other; but natural affection between families is common, even among dogs and birds. It is natural affection between others that is so much rarer.

God has given us the pattern for this, because he has, as it were, heard our sufferings from outside this dentist's surgery of a world, and has not been able to bear not being with us. More than that, he has not been able to bear not being us.

Just as my worry about my wife took her mind off her pain, so Christ's care for us reduces our pain. The mark of the Christian Church is or should be its identification with its Lord, and with each other. We know we ought not greedily to grab the loving sacrifice of Christ and at the same time hug to ourselves our houses and cars and incomes, like children trying hard not to let other children play with their toys.

Because the love of money is the root of all evil, we use almsgiving as a symbol of all our giving, of our acceptance that we owe each other natural love, and pay the debt as willingly as Christ gave his life. Making a gift sets us up, keeps us going, in the same way as prayer.

2

I do not want to give the impression that almsgiving matters only to the givers, and not to the recipients. Givers and recipients are bound up together, as I have explained. But it is important that we should be properly trained in almsgiving, as most of us are properly trained in courtesy. We may take a present to our hostess at a big party, and say thank you afterwards, without giving much more thought to the size of the present, or the elaborateness of the thanks, than she will. The symbol is much more important than the size.

Of course, a hostess is not a case of desperate need. Our desire to help the poor or sick may lead us to think harder about what we can manage to give; but the first and most important step is to establish the custom of giving.

When the Wise Men gave gifts to the baby in the stable, they gave things valuable in the sight of the poor people who received them, but they did not act out of any particularly charitable impulse: they were humbly offering tribute to a King, no doubt upon their knees. I like to think of those gifts as symbols of the Holy Trinity: gold the royal mystery of God's creation, myrrh the bitter mystery of the Son's suffering, and frankincense the sweet mystery of the Spirit's fellowship. Like all gifts to God, they are really gifts from God. In giving, all men receive, because the giving acknowledges our true relationship with God. The Samaritan woman gives water to Jesus, and finds she is receiving the water of baptism to a new life. As the *Alternative Service Book* says: 'All things come from you, and of your own do we give you.'

Of course, it is not mere giving that is to be sought, but giving in the right spirit. If we drive our cars at 60 miles an hour in a controlled area, and meet a policeman, it solves nothing to give him ten pounds. We shall certainly receive from him in return, but not in any pleasant sense. The right gift in that situation is humility, an admission that we are wrong and will do better in future. We may be booked, but are likely to be surprised at the kindness we receive, because we have acknowledged the truth of how we stand.

In all this, the amount we give is not necessarily in proportion to what we receive; otherwise the person who writes a cheque for a hundred pounds and puts it into the church collection would be guaranteed a hundred times as much happiness as the common run of one pounders. You cannot buy God, if only because what he has to give is out of all proportion to what we have to offer.

The question of what is acceptable to God is a difficult one. There are so many people who give sacrificially, yet never come near a church, and to whom we can have no idea of God's reaction, except to know that it is loving.

So our kind pagans may or may not be acceptable to God. It is not our concern to peer into people's hearts and sort them out for him. It is our own giving that should concern us; and even then we must never delight in imagining that we are doing better than others.

God has already given us the gold of creation and the myrrh of redemption. The frankincense of grace will come when we follow the logic of that great prayer in the 1662 prayer book, which says: 'Here we offer and present unto thee ourselves, our souls and bodies, to be a reasonable, holy, and lively sacrifice unto thee.' We heard it, or the A.S.B. equivalent, at our last Communion; and we shall hear it again at our next. Meanwhile, we have the opportunity to give alms.

LIGHT

1

'Let your light so shine before men, that they may see your good works, and glorify your Father which is in heaven.' So runs the Communion sentence before almsgiving; and one instantly envisages members of the congregation brandishing cheques and notes of high denomination before dropping them into the 'decent bason', or, more commonly, collecting bag.

Clearly, one envisages wrongly, for such a situation would be quite appalling. It would not be light that these wealthy show-offs would be shedding, but deep darkness. I fear there is a case for using some other sentence, in case the congregation should get hold of the wrong end of the stick.

In Matthew 5, from which the sentence comes, our Lord is urging his followers to let what they believe and how they behave be seen by everybody, and not hidden. That this is not an invitation to show off is demonstrated by the stories of the poor widow and the Pharisee and the publican. Sanctimoniousness is a sin that springs from pride, the root sin of all.

Undeniably, however, the line between publicly following your principles and showing off is a delicate one, especially as modesty is generally accepted as a virtue. Demonstrating modesty is very like not demonstrating at all.

I find the whole business of evangelism extremely difficult for that reason. The moment it becomes in the least aggressive, evangelism ceases to be effective; yet Christ commands it; and, beyond question, the need to set a decent example to others helps to keep us on the rails.

As so often, the first question to ask is how God himself handles the matter. Reticently, and elusively, I should say.

When the risen Christ returns to his disciples, there is remarkable confusion about his identity. Mary Magdalen finds this in the garden; so do the disciples at Emmaus; and Thomas had his problems, too. Later, when Peter and the rest are fishing, a person appears on the shore and hails them. He is admittedly some distance away, dressed like anybody else, and not speaking at his normal volume; but he is not recognised until he puts John and Peter on to a shoal of fish.

This suggests that Jesus was not unusual in build: he was not twenty stone, or four feet high, or specially tall. Nor, in his resurrected person, was he surrounded by weird light or given anything to suggest superhumanity.

Then, after the Ascension, he is gone, and the disciples are left in the same sort of state as our own, in a world where Jesus does not suddenly turn up and barbecue fish, or show us his wounds, or talk to us on an evening road.

It is as if man is placed in a shuttered house, round which the light and glory of God shine, but invisibly to us, except for the odd chink through the shutters, or a gleam on the face of some fellow-human, as Moses showed when he came down from Mount Sinai.

If this is how God's light shines, what does it tell us about how our light should shine? After all, God even hid his light from his own Son on the Cross and, before it, seems only to have given Jesus gleams. There is no ta-ra of trumpets and blaze of glory about the way he behaves; so why should we think of ourselves as making a great fuss?

So, abandoning the limited but useful metaphor about the shuttered house, how does God show us gleams? The first is the obvious way. You know God is there because what happens is typical of him. Peter knew Jesus was Jesus, because Jesus knew where the big fish were. The disciples at Emmaus knew him because of the way he blessed and broke bread. Thomas knew him by his suffering. We know him by sacraments, the outward and visible signs of something inward and spiritual. Returning to the dark house, we find some objects that seem to reflect the light we seek.

The second way God shows himself is inside ourselves. The Holy Spirit is in us, giving us inward certainty and comfort.

Thirdly, there is a book in the house that shines with a strange light, and that tells the vital story of the life of our Lord.

So we are back, as so often, to the Holy Trinity: showing forth God in creation, in the Spirit, and in the life of Jesus. There is the light we are given.

2

Evangelism is the shining of God's light for other people as God shines it for us. It is a duty commanded by Christ himself. It is essentially modest, in that it is not centred on the self of the evangelist. We do not say: 'Look at us', but rather: 'Look at the light'- in creation, in the Bible story, inside ourselves and others.

But first we have to understand the creature to whom we are speaking, and what happened when God first shone the light for him. Because love insisted that man must be free to go wrong, God was in a position not unlike that of an electrician wiring up a house. The electrician knows very well that later on the supply will be unsuitable to new demands, that bulbs will go at awkward times, that the son of the house will try to run two fires and an electric motor off a light socket, that plugs will be fitted up dangerously, and nails driven through the wiring; but for all this, he goes ahead and does the work, because he knows that on the whole the house will be lighted and heated.

Why, under such hazardous circumstances, did God go ahead and create man? There are answers to this question in the early Fathers, but I shall save it up for the Last Judgment. As I say, it is something to do with love. If man had no choice by which he could abuse things, he would be worse off than a battery hen, which can at least cluck, refuse food, or turn its head to left or right. If we were not able to choose at all, we should lose the joy of choosing a wife, a husband, a meal, a job: the sort of joy perhaps God had in creation.

I know this is not a complete answer; but any rate, we do have freedom; and we have more than that: when we do make a mess, we have what St Paul calls a second creation in Christ. Unlike the electrician, God did not just walk away and leave us: sticking to crude and barely acceptable terms, he gave us a sort of free maintenance contract.

Even there, we are free to say: 'No, thank you. I want no guarantee. I can manage for myself.' A lot of people say this, accepting the first creation, but not the second. This is where evangelism comes in.

If evangelism were merely a sales pitch for a maintenance contract, it would be only what I am afraid it sometimes becomes: a worldly routine to obtain power and money. Gently persuading people to accept the second creation has to be a joy, a sharing of God's own joy in creation. All of us who have seen children and friends setting about destroying themselves know the aching desire to help, and the joy when help is effective. This is our sharing in God's own work.

Here again, tact and common sense are vital. If you see a person misusing a vacuum cleaner, and spreading more dust than he gets up, you have three choices: to walk off and say: 'Silly fool!'; to empty the dusty bag; and to explain to the person how to empty it for himself. The second choice is a sort of charity, but only the third is evangelism, because it changes the person's life. You have created a chance that someone will be more sensible, and less dirty and lazy, than before; and thereby altered the course of the world.

But the knowledge was not yours. It was there in the instruction booklet, written by the makers. Your task is only that of an interpreter; and so is the task of an evangelist. You are helping to make things work as they were originally designed to.

3

When I was a boy at school, they made me something called Sacristan. I had to go into the school chapel on Saturday nights, while the rest were doing their prep, and get the sanctuary ready for Communion. On a winter night, it was a very silent sort of place, approached along a corridor full of tribal masks and curious objects from Africa, donated by devoted Old Boys.

The chapel was very dimly lit, and seemed to possess a life of its own; because the old wooden pews, expanding and contracting in the primitive central heating, used to creak and snap, as if they were full of creatures, crawling in and out under cover, waiting to get at me. By the time I had finished, I was pretty scared, and would hurry out of chapel without looking back.

One Saturday, the electricity was cut off. If it had happened while I was in the chapel, I should have been gibbering with terror, but mercifully I had not started, and the Chaplain gave me a single lighted candle to work by.

I cannot tell you how comforting the candle was. It lighted everything in that big building, and seemed to keep at bay all my fears and fancies. Now, you are thinking, he is going to quote from the *Merchant of Venice* and talk about the light of Christ in the darkness of the world. Yes, certainly; and to quote our Lord: 'No follower of mine shall wander in the dark' and 'Do you bring in a candle to put it under a mattress?' But above all to stress how one very small source of light makes such an enormous difference. As a young lad, I was like a primitive savage, a fertile ground for superstition, and nervousness, and uncertainty; yet that one gleam gave me the confidence of a civilised man, more so than the brash glare of electricity. There was a beauty and a warmth about it, somehow.

So, where crime, or drink, or drugs, or unhappy marriages or non-marriages have brought a person to breakdown, then long and patient analysis, explanation, or delving into the dark past, may bring less relief than the single light of Christ, suffering himself to be consumed to give us hope and confidence. Again, there is a beauty and a warmth about it, somehow.

That light is in our hand; but it is not our light.

4

Showing our light may make all the difference to someone, or to many; but the very thought of it summons up uncomfortable images of evangelists knocking on doors and demanding: 'Are you saved?' The steamy atmosphere of militant evangelism is not for many of us; but flowers grow even in steamy atmospheres, and God may use the brutal challenge, the emotional testimony, the shouts of 'Hallelujah', as he certainly uses 'the high-embowed roof With antic pillars massy proof, And storied windows richly dight, Casting a dim religious light;' and the accompanying quiet prayerfulness. There are varieties of function in the Body of Christ, and I dare say we each have our special sort of ability to communicate.

For most, it is more important to be, than to try to communicate. Power over others soon becomes abused, where it is consciously exercised. The root of true leadership lies in doing something in such a way that others want to do it too. Even a person who has no gift of leadership at all is capable of behaving kindly and looking happy about it, and of firmly refusing to become involved in anything dishonourable.

He is in a real sense following our Lord's command to preach the gospel to all nations.

As for a conventional preacher, such as myself, he is only too capable of misusing his light in the way you misuse a torch, by shining it in people's faces and confusing them, or by hitting them over the head with it, or using too weak a battery, or pointing it at himself. He is there to point, as it were, to a picture and draw attention to its features. He may communicate enthusiasm, but it needs to be genuine and not forced. The light that illuminates his subject may also illuminate him, but he should not seek to achieve that end.

Air and light are two marvellous elements in which we live. One we breathe in common; the other enables us to see clearly who and what we are. For air, read grace. For the light of the sun, read the light of God. We reflect both, whether we mean to or not.

MORALITY

1

Preaching morality is all too easy; so easy that modern preachers feel the need either to complicate it or, more often, to transform it into a sort of alternative system. One frequently hears quoted Augustine's advice to love God, and do as you like; as if this abolishes not only conventional morality, but also the advice of both Jesus and St Paul to follow worldly authority.

Clearly, their advice ceases to apply wherever worldly authority demands a rejection of God; but the occasions when we are faced with this sort of dilemma are fewer than zealots believe. It may even be that we owe more respect than we usually pay to some of those Germans who were slow to oppose the Nazis; though we are right to respect above all those like Dietrich Bonhoeffer who saw when the law of man had overstepped the wide bounds it must be allowed.

It is all too easy to be 'agin the Government'. Trendy clerics have made a cult of it since the Sixties; and although it is perfectly permissible to express opinions on policy, it is destructive of worldly order to give the impression that a Christian is a member of an alternative society, constantly dealing direct with a higher power than the higher powers. Every time we talk about the distinction between the world and the Kingdom of God, we risk giving the impression that God is not interested in how we run our daily lives.

If the world does not matter, why were we put into it? One of the objects of religious teaching is to tell us how to live in the world. Of course God is our highest authority; but we have no right to dismiss all inferior authorities as the emissaries of Satan, and go bouncing to the top every time.

Bonhoeffer saw his world as the world of the Old Testament. He could not find the Nazis in the New, and concluded that the New Testament was a pattern towards which we strive, while the Old speaks of our actual condition. 'We live on the next to last word,' he wrote, 'and believe on the last, don't we?'

The Jewish Law was formed to deal with Old Testamentary conditions; and Jesus made it clear he had not come to destroy the Law, but to fulfil it. The grace he brings is intended to complete the Law, not to replace it. It also completes, not replaces, all human laws. Jesus could have resisted the human laws that led to his crucifixion; but he did not.

Laws are made to prevent nastinesses that happened in the unregulated past. This is true whether you are studying Leviticus or the Law of England. Our Civil Law is founded on all the frauds and robberies and murders of past times, and includes a large element of Case Law; that means that records are kept of the way judges apply the Law, so that their example can be followed in the future. No one should feel in a superior sort of way that God offers him a better way of doing things. Even so, we have to be on the lookout that the law is not being perverted, so that its provisions are serving as instruments of oppression. That is what had happened with the Jewish Law.

Even God can be made to seem an instrument of oppression by those extreme people who reckon he guides them in every detail of their lives, and will not acknowledge lesser authorities. Where we eat because we are hungry, they eat because God tells them; where we marry because we are in love, they marry under a strict religious direction. We know that God made food and marriage, hunger and sex, and are happy to follow second causes; they will not acknowledge the authority of second causes. They are not really God's rebels; just rebels. God, by his Son's conduct and precept, does not want us to be rebels. It seems to have been Judas who wanted to rebel; until the moment when he turned to the Law as an instrument of oppression.

2

So far, I have not distinguished between law and morality. Of course, one must do so. Morality demands that we obey the law, but it demands a lot more as well. When Jesus talks about morality, he is mainly referring to that. The law may tell us to do something; Jesus tells us to go beyond it, and do more. He is speaking in terms of the Jewish Law, but what he says applies equally to human law. A ban on parking, except on a broken yellow line, has at its root the need to keep the streets unobstructed. If we are not to be legalistic, sticking to every jot of our rights, we need to keep in mind the spirit underlying the ban. This may well lead us not to park, even where it is allowed, when we shall obstruct the street. Insisting on our rights is legalism, and a sort of oppression.

Paul talks more about good behaviour than Jesus, because he is coping with the new Church, which has given rise to all sorts of problems. He has to fight against fornicating, sorcery, quarrelling, and orgies, things, however legal, that are contrary to the Christian Way. Human law, which is against such as murderers, thieves, and false accusers, is his ally, assisting him in the Way, and giving him space to deal with the rest. Where the Law does not operate, the Spirit is needed as a guide to right behaviour.

In our day, the Spirit may seem to speak with an uncertain voice. There is little doubt that the early Church condemned homosexuality, whereas a growing number of Christians today feel that it is permissible. Slavery is now thought to be intolerable, whereas it was tolerated in New Testament times. What has happened is that liberal ideas have won a considerable victory. The clergyman who hunted in Victorian times was felt to be going a bit far, not so much because he watched foxes torn to bits, but because he ought to have been occupying his time better. Today, it is the nature of his occupation that attracts criticism; whereas if he stands among the hunt saboteurs, even those in favour of hunting feel obscurely that he is in the right place.

Jesus himself is seen to be talking like a liberal, and his fiercer remarks are ignored. His message is interpreted as: do as you like, so long as no one is obviously damaged by your behaviour.

There are three things to be said about this: that it is only too often applied hypocritically; that it is a half truth; and that it substitutes one inadequate law for another. If our age is to survive, these three facts have got to be studied, understood, and digested.

3

First of all, as to hypocrisy: of the Christian variety, that is. How easily we drift into a way of life in which we take our own decisions, and then expect whoever runs the universe to tidy up after us, to make it all right. We change a job, or move house, or embark on some new enterprise, telling ourselves: 'The Lord is calling us to do this.' Maybe he does; but not always. Sometimes we are rationalizing our own selfishness.

A young rascal with no thought in his head but enjoying himself and avoiding hard work goes off abroad on a service scheme, and hears us all say in our innocence: 'What a splendid, heroic, caring young man!' This convinces him that his selfishness is saintliness. Such are the ways of God that sometimes it even becomes so.

Or we apply for a job with more money and better working conditions, talking piously about being 'called to a wider sphere.' So, time and again, we are tempted to whistle up God to approve of our running our life by our own interest and wishes.

In this way, a new sort of permissiveness grows. The young people who want to cohabit elevate what they are doing into a new Christian insight. What does it matter, anyway, if they are not harming anyone? Their hypocrisy lies in the fact that they shut their eyes to the possibility that they are harming each other, their parents, their future spouses, even society as a whole.

Next, as to the principle of not harming anyone being a half-truth anyway. The principle is most convincingly based on our Lord's command that we should love our neighbour as ourself. Although this can hardly be called a half-truth, it is necessary to point out that the first and greatest commandment is to love God; and also that loving our neighbour as we love ourselves does imply loving ourselves. This is not in the sense of vanity, but as self-care, which St James calls keeping oneself unspotted from the world.

This does not merely mean we must not harm ourselves: most of us watch out for that. Rather it means that we must understand fully what spiritual harm is before we set about rewriting Christianity.

Lastly, I must return to what I said about following the law, whether it be the Jewish Law or some moral law like that about doing no harm to others. The whole point of what Jesus says is that we must go beyond law into the realm of the Spirit that lies behind the law. The law urges us to go one pace, so we should go two.

This is well shown in St Paul's careful instructions in Romans as to how to avoid upsetting those who do not eat meat. You may justly feel, he says, that eating meat is lawful; but if others do not feel so, refrain from it. This sort of self-restraint is badly needed in an age when public and private behaviour are frequently confused, and new moral principles are announced, to justify upsetting those who hold to more established ones.

So the advice to love God, and do as you please, does not in fact amount to doing what you fancy, as long as it harms nobody. It extends to understanding what loving God really involves, and is not something easily worked out in the back of a taxi.

4

I do not want to leave the subject of morality with an attack on modern attitudes. The gift of God to man is not so much the power to take as the power to give, and it is important that we should see our behaviour as a positive contribution to the Kingdom.

My first suggestion is that we get our responses to stimuli as right as we can. I have always sympathised with the jealous elder brother in the Parable of the Prodigal Son. Where he went obviously wrong was in his immediate response. The story of Jesus healing the ten lepers is another case in point. They were given the stimulus of being healed, but only one found the response of coming back to say thank you. The others had different responses to the fact of being cured, of which we know nothing: one perhaps wanted to get married, and another wanted to enrol for an apprenticeship, and another to celebrate; but if any had had a Victorian nanny, he would have been in no doubt what to do first: say thank you to the gentleman. The training of stock responses is very important. When omitted, it can cause great trouble, not excluding war between nations.

A car knocked me off my bicycle one day in a Cambridge street, and I was momentarily too shaken to tell the driver he was an irresponsible and clumsy so-and-so. To my surprise, instead of asking me what I thought I was doing, weaving all over the road, he was led by my mildness to collapse into a remorseful jelly. What could have been a slanging match, finishing in court, became a question of care for the injured. Purely by mistake, I had stimulated a different response. It was like when a dog turns over and puts his paws in the air; and all the other dogs are gentle with him.

We have to train ourselves to a stock response of love and kindness. When Paul urges us to be 'in Christ', he implies that, in any new situation, we should put our hands automatically in the position of blessing and acceptance rather than of pugnacity.

The other training we badly need is in recovering the concept of honour. The word has a rectangular, old-fashioned air that instantly arouses suspicions. If it means anything to you, it probably means keeping your word.

In fact, whole ages have been founded on this idea, which signified the whole worth of a man, seen through the eyes of other people. The pagan idea was taken over by Christianity and applied to God himself, who was not content just to be good, but insisted on coming to earth and doing good in the sight of all nations and ages. Consequently, we too should hope to live, not in a sort of withdrawn, sinless state, but in a positive manner, which the world would recognise was good. Even monasticism satisfied this requirement.

When Antony calls Brutus an honourable man, he means not only that Brutus has a fine reputation, but that his reputation is justified. To be honourable, you have to score on both these counts. If you are a devil, and everybody believes you to be a saint, like Mr Pecksniff in *Martin Chuzzlewit*, you are not honourable, but a hypocrite.

It was a constant fear among the educated classes for centuries that they would be thought less than they were. They would go to absurd lengths, such as duelling, to avoid this. I remember two firm friends, in an obscure seventeenth century play, fighting a duel merely for honour's sake. One was killed, together with both their seconds, and the audience was supposed to applaud. This sort of nonsense caused people to shy away from the word 'honour' about 150 years ago, and substitute 'respectability'. This ridiculous concept died in the middle of the twentieth century. Instead, seeming good has ceased to have its former importance. It is mostly the older people who twitch the curtain, and say: 'There's the policeman at No.12' or 'There's the curate calling on Miss Jones again'. As for Miss Jones, she seems to delight in giving the wrong impression.

Of course, caring about what people say easily becomes hypocrisy; but not caring about what they say may be just as bad a fault. We have to recapture the idea that we are encompassed about with a great cloud of witnesses; that most of our life, sooner or later, will be found to have been led in public. What we do in secret is likely to emerge to some degree, at some time, not only before the eyes of God, who has seen it all already, but before the eyes of our fellows.

Our predecessors knew that good and bad were not private matters. Honour is always at stake.

Honour will be satisfied; and the honour of being seen to do what is right at all costs, which is the honour of Christ, is worth having; if anything is worth having.

CONCLUSION

It was a passage in a fourteenth century book called *The Scale of Perfection*, by an English monk called Walter Hilton, that stopped me worrying.

'A good man living in the world ... does ... good acts of mercy for the love of God. He will have his reward in heaven, not for these actions in themselves, but for the goodwill and charity given him by God which moved him to do them ... Another man may do the same good actions out of vanity, to win honour and praise from the world and to gain a good name for himself; he also has his reward here. In ... these instances the determining factor is that one has charity, and the other has none. Which is the one and which the other God knows, and he alone.'

That last sentence is shattering, and rather spikes the guns of anyone who writes as I have written. The point is that God is in charge, and not we ourselves. Our problem is with ourselves, and not with others. Anyone who writes or speaks for others, as I do, needs divine help and permission; which is why preachers give an ascription before and after their sermons. My Preface and Conclusion must be taken as that.

Among all the gifts that God gives us there are some that are brighter than others. St Paul tells us that whereas other gifts shine for a little, and become tarnished, three will last for ever: faith, hope, and love.

I do not have to tell you which is the greatest of these. My hope is that all we do may catch at least a little of its reflected light.

PAUL GRIFFIN

Paul (1922–2012) was a soldier, scholar, teacher, poet and Lay Reader in the Church of England.

Educated at Framlingham College, he served with the Gurkhas and Chindits in India and Burma during World War II. He read English at St Catharine's College, Cambridge going on to teach at Uppingham. From there he became Principal of the English School in Nicosia and, returning to the UK after independence in 1960, Head of Aldenham School. Latterly he returned to Cambridge to run a language school.

He became a Lay Reader, being licensed by the diocese of St Albans and then St Edmundsbury and Ipswich, working across rural East Suffolk.

In retirement he returned to his first love of writing and produced a string of poems, parodies and articles which were widely published. Many of the serious ones related to his strong faith.

He was particularly proud of winning, on three occasions, the Cambridge University Seatonian Prize for an extended poem on a religious theme.

www.ingramcontent.com/pod-product-compliance
Lightning Source LLC
Chambersburg PA
CBHW060630030426
42337CB00018B/3296